POSTWAR AMERICA
THE KOREAN WAR

by Brienna Rossiter

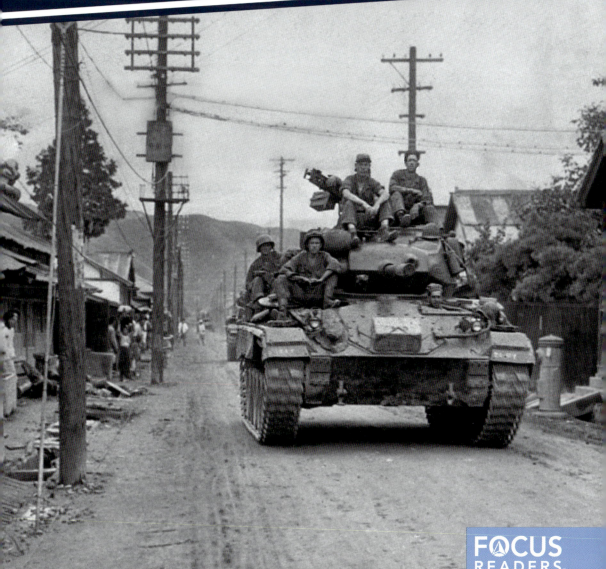

FOCUS READERS®
NAVIGATOR

WWW.FOCUSREADERS.COM

Copyright © 2024 by Focus Readers®, Mendota Heights, MN 55120. All rights reserved. No part of this book may be reproduced or utilized in any form or by any means without written permission from the publisher.

Focus Readers is distributed by North Star Editions:
sales@northstareditions.com | 888-417-0195

Produced for Focus Readers by Red Line Editorial.

Content Consultant: Liping Bu, PhD, Professor of History, Alma College

Photographs ©: AP Images, cover, 1, 9, 16–17, 28; US Army Signal Corps/AP Images, 4–5; Red Line Editorial, 7; Korean Central News Agency/Korea News Service/AP Images, 10–11; Hulton-Deutsch Collection/Corbis Historical/Getty Images, 13; US Army/AP Images, 14; Jim Pringle/AP Images, 19, George Sweers/AP Images, 21, 24–25; Bettmann/Getty Images, 23; CIH/AP Images, 27

Library of Congress Cataloging-in-Publication Data
Names: Rossiter, Brienna, author.
Title: The Korean War / by Brienna Rossiter.
Description: Mendota Heights, MN : Focus Readers, [2024] | Series: Postwar
  America | Includes bibliographical references and index. | Audience:
  Grades 4-6
Identifiers: LCCN 2023033092 (print) | LCCN 2023033093 (ebook) | ISBN
  9798889980414 (hardcover) | ISBN 9798889980841 (paperback) | ISBN
  9798889981657 (ebook pdf) | ISBN 9798889981275 (ebook other)
Subjects: LCSH: Korean War, 1950-1953--Juvenile literature. | Korean War,
  1950-1953--United States--Juvenile literature.
Classification: LCC DS918 .R67 2024 (print) | LCC DS918 (ebook) | DDC
  951.904/2--dc23/eng/20230809
LC record available at https://lccn.loc.gov/2023033092
LC ebook record available at https://lccn.loc.gov/2023033093

Printed in the United States of America
Mankato, MN
012024

ABOUT THE AUTHOR
Brienna Rossiter is a writer and editor who lives in Minnesota. She loves learning about history.

TABLE OF CONTENTS

CHAPTER 1

A Divided Country 5

CHAPTER 2

Back and Forth 11

CHAPTER 3

Stalemate 17

VOICES FROM THE PAST

Prisoners of War 22

CHAPTER 4

Uneasy Peace 25

Focus on the Korean War • 30
Glossary • 31
To Learn More • 32
Index • 32

CHAPTER 1

A DIVIDED COUNTRY

World War II (1939–1945) ended with Japan's surrender. However, a new conflict was already brewing. During World War II, the United States and the Soviet Union had been **allies**. After the war, relations between them grew tense. The Soviet Union supported **Communism**. The United States opposed

By the end of 1949, the United States and the Soviet Union both had nuclear weapons. These bombs could destroy entire cities.

this idea. Both countries tried to spread their views. This conflict became known as the Cold War. It shaped many decisions made after World War II.

For example, Japan's **colonies** were set free after the war. Korea was one of them. Japan had taken it over in 1910. Now, Korea needed a new government. Several groups wanted to lead it. Some of them supported Communism. Others wanted to make Korea more like the West.

The United States and the Soviet Union split Korea into two zones. The country was divided at the 38th parallel. This latitude line ran midway through Korea. The Soviet Union would control the area north of the line. The United States would take charge south of it. The split was not meant to be permanent. But in 1948, two separate governments were created.

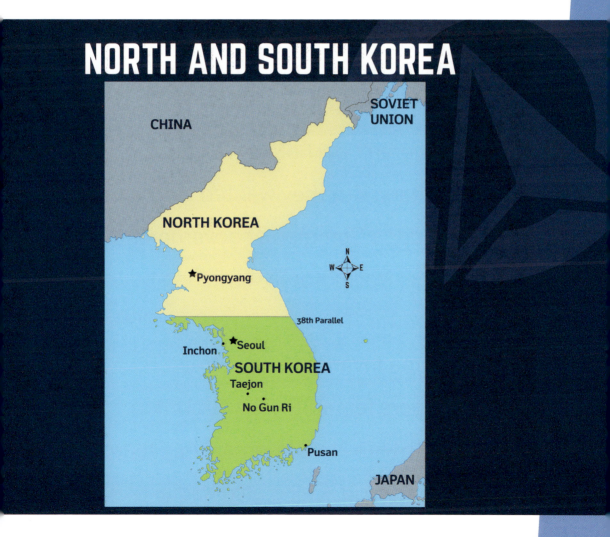

The Democratic People's Republic of Korea was set up in the north. It supported Communism. In the south, the United Nations (UN) helped set up the Republic of Korea (ROK).

In the late 1940s, Communist **guerrillas** attacked in the south. These fighters weren't part of North Korea's main military. But they wanted to unite Korea under a Communist government. Meanwhile, North Korea worked to build military power. Then, on June 25, 1950, North Korea invaded the south.

US leaders feared the Soviet Union would side with North Korea. They feared China would, too. China also had a

A group of US soldiers arrive in South Korea in July 1950.

Communist government. So, US President Harry S. Truman urged the UN to act.

The UN told North Korea to stop the invasion. But North Korea kept going. So, the UN called for countries to help defend South Korea. US soldiers made up most of the UN troops. They began fighting on June 30. Only five years after the end of World War II, a new war had begun.

CHAPTER 2

BACK AND FORTH

North Korea's forces were called the Korean People's Army (KPA). They reached South Korea's capital, Seoul, in just three days. The KPA had help from the Soviet Union. Meanwhile, the ROK army lacked numbers and supplies. So did the newly arrived UN troops. For much of the summer, they struggled to

North Korean tanks enter Seoul in June 1950.

slow the KPA's invasion. But by August, they started having more success.

The combined ROK and UN forces were known as the United Nations Command (UNC). Most of their supplies were sent through a port at Pusan. The KPA tried to advance toward it. However, the UNC pushed them back.

Meanwhile, US general Douglas MacArthur was planning a surprise attack. He sent UNC troops north to Inchon. There, they would make a landing from the sea. This plan was risky. The water was full of explosives. And Inchon was close to Seoul. The KPA still controlled that city.

Civilians walk through the ruined streets of Inchon after US forces took the city.

MacArthur's attack was a success. UNC soldiers took over Inchon on September 15. And by September 25, they had retaken Seoul.

At this point, US leaders convinced the UNC to change its goals. Before, the UNC had only wanted to stop the KPA. Now, the UNC also aimed to reunite Korea. The UNC created plans to invade the north.

 Thousands of people fled Seoul before North Korean and Chinese forces retook the city.

China warned that it would join the fighting if UNC troops crossed the 38th parallel. But in October, UNC forces invaded anyway. As promised, China sent troops. These troops fought alongside the KPA. Together, they drove the UNC all the way back to the 38th parallel. Then they kept going.

In January 1951, Communist soldiers retook Seoul. But in March, UNC forces took it back. After that, they pushed the Communist soldiers back to the 38th parallel.

BRUTAL FIGHTING

Communist soldiers shot or captured many people as they moved through South Korea. In the city of Taejon, they killed 5,000 people. UNC forces killed **civilians**, too. Near the village of No Gun Ri, American troops killed people who were fleeing the war. And the ROK army often killed people who were thought to be Communists.

CHAPTER 3

STALEMATE

Fighting continued throughout 1951. But neither side got much past the 38th parallel. Each time one side made progress, the other pushed back. Both sides began to change their goals. Winning the war and reuniting Korea no longer seemed possible. Leaders considered making a truce.

US troops used parachutes to drop into territory held by North Korea.

General MacArthur disliked this new approach. So, President Truman replaced him. General Matthew Ridgway took charge of the UNC troops in April 1951. Soon after, leaders from both sides began peace talks. By October 1951, they had agreed to keep Korea divided at the 38th parallel. A **demilitarized zone** (DMZ) would be set up there. It would separate the north from the south.

However, peace talks stalled soon after that. The two sides disagreed about what to do with prisoners of war (POWs). During the fighting, both sides had captured many soldiers. Usually, countries exchange POWs when a war

UNC forces send captured Chinese soldiers to a prison camp in 1951.

ends. But some people held in UNC prison camps were actually from South Korea. The KPA had captured people and forced them to fight. These people didn't want to go to North Korea. Some Chinese soldiers also didn't want to return home.

Truman said no POWs held by the UNC would be sent back if they didn't want

19

to go. But this meant all POWs had to be screened. The UNC had to find out which POWs wanted to stay. This process proved to be very complicated.

Meanwhile, in the south, guerrilla warfare continued. Communist soldiers hid in the mountains. They attacked

SPIES

Part of POW screening involved making sure people weren't lying. They might have been trying to stay in South Korea as spies. In several places, Communist spies were able to get into the UNC's camps. They disrupted the screening process. They also started fights in several camps. Many prisoners were killed. So were some guards.

Near the end of the war, fighting often focused on controlling hills and ridges.

towns and UNC soldiers. Regular battles also continued. Both sides hoped gaining territory could help them get a better peace deal. The battle lines didn't move much. But both sides suffered heavy losses.

21

VOICES FROM THE PAST

PRISONERS OF WAR

More than 7,000 American soldiers were held as prisoners during the Korean War. Robert Fletcher was one. His unit was captured in November 1950. Then they were forced to march for weeks. They received little food. Guards shot people who fell behind. And the weather was extremely cold. "We had no covers or blankets," Fletcher recalled. "You'd go to sleep, and when you woke up, two or three guys would be frozen to death."[1]

The cold and hunger continued when they reached a POW camp. POWs also had to attend "education sessions." Captors tried to make them convert to Communism. Black soldiers like Fletcher were especially targeted. The sessions focused on the mistreatment Black Americans faced back home. "The Chinese knew the history

During the Korean War, POWs faced sickness, starvation, torture, and freezing cold.

of the United States very well, and they played the game with it," Fletcher said.[2]

Fletcher spent nearly three years in the camp. He was released after the war ended. But many were not so fortunate. Approximately 40 percent of American POWs died.

1. David P. Cline. *Twice Forgotten: African Americans and the Korean War, an Oral History*. Chapel Hill: University of North Carolina Press, 2021. Print. Page 260.
2. Cline. Page 264.

23

CHAPTER 4

UNEASY PEACE

Dwight D. Eisenhower became the new US president in January 1953. Peace talks continued. But so did debates about POWs. Then, in March 1953, Soviet leader Joseph Stalin died. The new Soviet leader wanted peace in Korea. China and the KPA knew they couldn't keep fighting without Soviet support. So, they agreed

Soldiers and civilians continued to die while leaders debated ways to end the war.

to voluntary **repatriation**. Starting in April, some POWs were exchanged.

Meanwhile, Communist and UNC forces were still fighting. Plus, South Korea needed to agree to peace. Its leader, Syngman Rhee, had not done so. But he did after the United States promised aid to South Korea.

On July 27, leaders from the United States, China, and North Korea signed the agreement. Fighting stopped after that. However, no one from South Korea ever signed the agreement. For this reason, the war never technically ended.

From 1953 on, Korea remained divided near the 38th parallel. The DMZ split the

US general Mark Clark signs the agreement to stop fighting in July 1953.

two countries. Forces from North Korea and the UNC guarded it. People were not allowed to cross.

Borders were back where they had started in 1945. But the war had many lasting impacts. One was the devastating loss of life. Approximately three million people died. Most were civilians.

 US forces used more bombs in North Korea than they used in all of Asia during World War II.

Bombing by US planes destroyed much of North Korea. The bombs often used napalm. This chemical started huge fires. The war damaged land in South Korea as well. Thousands of people lost their homes. Approximately 15,000 Koreans left their country and settled in the United States.

The war also shaped US foreign policy. The US military continued to take an active role in conflicts around the world. American soldiers were sent to many other countries. This pattern of getting involved continues to the present day.

KOREAN GOVERNMENTS

Kim Il Sung ruled North Korea from 1948 until his death in 1994. After that, his son and then grandson ruled. All three were **authoritarian** leaders who kept a strong military. South Korea was meant to be a republic, where people voted to elect a president. But the 1960s and 1970s saw several periods of military rule. In 1988, South Korea began holding peaceful elections again. By the 2010s, it had one of the strongest **economies** in the world.

FOCUS ON
THE KOREAN WAR

Write your answers on a separate piece of paper.

1. Write a paragraph summarizing the main ideas of Chapter 2.

2. Do you think the United States should take sides in conflicts that happen in other countries? Why or why not?

3. When did the Korean War begin?
   - **A.** 1950
   - **B.** 1951
   - **C.** 1953

4. How could a country get a better peace deal by taking more territory near the end of a war?
   - **A.** The other side might refuse to take part in peace talks.
   - **B.** The other side might fear losing and agree to more demands.
   - **C.** The other side might get angry and make poor decisions.

Answer key on page 32.

GLOSSARY

allies
Nations or people that are on the same side during a war.

authoritarian
Putting the power of the government above the freedoms of the people.

civilians
People who are not in the military.

colonies
Areas that are taken over and ruled by another country.

Communism
A political idea that calls for all property to be owned by the public.

demilitarized zone
An area where all military forces are removed.

economies
Systems of goods, services, money, and jobs.

guerrillas
Fighters who use surprise attacks and are not part of a regular army.

repatriation
The process of sending people back to their home country.

TO LEARN MORE

BOOKS

Berglund, Bruce. *Sergeant Reckless Braves the Battlefield: Heroic Korean War Horse*. North Mankato, MN: Capstone Press, 2023.

Gaines, Ann Graham. *Harry S. Truman*. Mankato, MN: The Child's World, 2020.

Makos, Adam. *Devotion: An Epic Story of Heroism and Friendship, Adapted for Young Adults*. New York: Delacorte Press, 2022.

NOTE TO EDUCATORS

Visit **www.focusreaders.com** to find lesson plans, activities, links, and other resources related to this title.

INDEX

China, 7–8, 14, 25–26

Eisenhower, Dwight D., 25

Fletcher, Robert, 22–23

Inchon, 7, 12–13

MacArthur, Douglas, 12–13, 18

prisoners of war, 18–20, 22–23, 25–26

Rhee, Syngman, 26
Ridgway, Matthew, 18

Seoul, 7, 11–13, 15
Soviet Union, 5–8, 11, 25
Stalin, Joseph, 25

Truman, Harry S., 9, 18–19

Answer Key: 1. Answers will vary; **2.** Answers will vary; **3.** A; **4.** B